Go get it!

7 Principles to Live a Legacy
Participant Guide

By

Chip Baker

2025

Woodz Worx Publishing

Copyright © 2025 by Chip Baker

All rights reserved. This book or any portion thereof may not be reproduced or used in any manner whatsoever without the express written permission of the publisher except for the use of brief quotations in a book review or scholarly journal.

First Printing: 2025

ISBN: 978-1-967464-44-9

Ordering Information:

Special discounts are available on quantity purchases by corporations, associations, educators, and others. For details, contact the publisher at the email listed below.

U.S. trade bookstores and wholesalers:

Please contact:
chipbakertsc@gmail.com

Introduction

This guide is designed to emphasize what you should learn from the book and videos. As you work through the material take the time to fill in all the blanks. Work through each section and apply the principles in your life. As you do this, your awareness of your actions to live and leave a legacy will grow.

Goals

Goal 1

<u>Live a Purpose-Driven Life</u>: Identify your core values and principles and develop a personal mission statement that aligns with the principle of being GROUNDED, enabling you to live a life of clarity and purpose.

Goal 2

<u>Cultivate a Positive Mindset</u>: Learn to embrace a mindset of possibility and develop a growth mindset, applying the principle of being OPTIMISTIC, to overcome obstacles and achieve your goals, and practice GRATITUDE by reflecting on your daily experiences.

Goal 3

<u>Build a Supportive Community</u>: Create a plan to surround yourself with people and environments that fuel your growth, applying the principle of ENVIRONMENTS, and develop strategies to maintain a supportive network, leveraging TRUST and TENACITY.

Goal 4

<u>Create a Lasting Legacy</u>: Develop a plan to turn your daily habits into a lasting impact, applying the 7 principles of legacy living, including living with INTENTIONS, to become the example others follow and leave a lasting legacy, and reflect on how you can embody the principles in your life.

After you complete this training, it will serve as a helpful reference guide as you consider your legacy. Go get it!

Table of Contents

Introduction	iii
Goals	iv
The Power of G.O.G.E.T.I.T.	1
Grounded: Stay Rooted in Your Values and Principles	5
Optimistic: Embrace a Mindset of Possibility	13
Gratitude: Cultivate Appreciation for the Present	21
Environments: Surround Yourself with What Fuels Your Growth	29
Tenacity: Persevere in the Face of Challenges	37
Intentions: Live with Clarity and Purpose	45
Trust: Believe in Yourself and the Process	53
Putting It All Together	61
The Go Get It Principles	67
About The Author	69
Answers	71

Go get it!

The Power of G.O.G.E.T.I.T.

"The secret to living a legacy is living with intention and purpose."

Have you ever wondered what it takes to leave a meaningful _____? A legacy that not only shapes your own life but leaves a lasting impact on the world around you.

The **G.O.G.E.T.I.T. Blueprint** is a powerful set of seven principles that, when embraced, will help you build a life full of

_____, _____ and _____ _____.

"I've never seen a house built from the roof down."

Each principle in the G.O.G.E.T.I.T. Blueprint is essential in weaving together the

_____ of your legacy.

It's not just about achieving _____; it's about the way you live, think, and act. These principles create an unbreakable connection between you and your

dreams, guiding you on your journey to _____.

"It's life changing to change lives."

Go get it!

Reflection Questions:

1. What does legacy mean to you?

2. List 3 legacy traits that influence others in a positive way.

Reflections

Reflections

Grounded: Stay Rooted in Your Values and Principles

1. Grounded: Stay Rooted in Your _____ and _____.

"Inner peace allows you to enter peace."

Being grounded means staying true to who you are. It's about having a solid foundation that keeps you anchored even when life gets challenging. The most successful people are those who know what they stand for, and they live by their values regardless of the circumstances.

Why It's Important: Being grounded gives you...

_____

_____

_____

It helps you make decisions from a place of integrity and keeps you focused on your _____ _____ _____.

"When you have core values you are always deeply rooted."

10 Actions to Help You Stay Grounded

Staying grounded is an ongoing practice. To help you build and maintain a solid foundation, here are 10 actionable steps you can take:

1. Meditate: Regular mindfulness practice reduces stress and increases self-awareness.

2. Journaling: Reflect on your thoughts, emotions, and experiences to process and release them.

3. Gratitude practice: Focus on the positive aspects of your day, no matter how small.

4. Spend time outdoors: Connect with nature, breathe fresh air, and recharge.

5. Walk or exercise: Physical activity helps reduce stress and boosts your mood.

6. Prioritize sleep: Adequate rest rejuvenates both your body and mind.

7. Healthy eating: Nourish your body with balanced, whole foods for better energy and well-being.

8. Deep breathing exercises: Focus on your breath to calm anxiety and center your mind.

9. Grounding activities: Engage in comforting activities or other hobbies that bring you peace.

10. Nurture relationships: Surround yourself with positive, supportive people who uplift you.

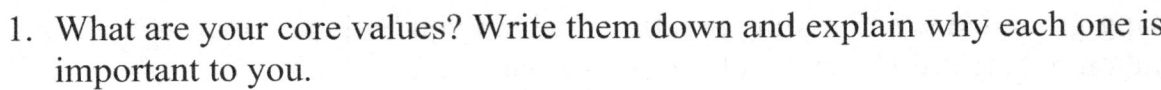

Reflection Questions:

1. What are your core values? Write them down and explain why each one is important to you.

2. Reflect on a recent challenge you faced. How did your core values help you navigate the situation?

3. Which of the 10 actions for staying grounded do you already practice? Which ones would you like to incorporate into your daily routine?

4. How do you define inner peace, and how can you cultivate it in your life?

Go get it!

Action Steps:

Identify Your Core Values: Which of the core values will you apply in your life?

Create a Personal Mission Statement: Define your purpose. What are you here to do?

Evaluate your mastery of The Grounded Principle. Rate Yourself 1-10 _____

Go get it!

Reflections

Reflections

Optimistic: Embrace a Mindset of Possibility

Go get it!

2. Optimistic: Embrace a _____ of Possibility

"The optimist sees the donut, the pessimist sees the hole."

Optimism is the _____ that no matter the challenge, there is always a _____.

By embracing an optimistic mindset, you fill your journey with hope and excitement. Optimism is the fuel that keeps you moving forward even when the path is _____.

Why It's Important: Optimism opens you up to _____ and allows you to see the potential in every situation.

It attracts positivity and keeps you _____.

"My blood type is Be Positive."

How to Cultivate Optimism: 10 Key Actions

Optimism is not something you're born with—it's a skill that can be cultivated. Here are 10 actionable steps to help you shift toward a more positive, solution-oriented mindset:

1. Practice Positive Self-Talk: Start by speaking kindly to yourself. Acknowledge your strengths and accomplishments. Challenge negative thoughts with affirmations and encouraging statements.

2. Reframe Negative Thoughts: When you catch yourself thinking negatively, pause and ask: "Is there another way to look at this?" Replace pessimistic thoughts with more hopeful, positive perspectives.

3. Focus on the Present: Let go of worries about the past or future. Focus on what you can control in the present moment and engage fully in each task or experience.

4. Keep a Gratitude Journal: Record three things you're grateful for each day. It could be as simple as a cup of coffee or a kind gesture from someone. Gratitude shifts your focus toward the positive.

5. Share Gratitude with Others: Express appreciation to those who make a positive impact in your life. Let others know that you value and acknowledge their presence.

6. Prioritize Sleep and Exercise: Physical health is directly tied to mental well-being. Regular physical activity and sufficient sleep improve mood, energy, and overall resilience.

7. Nourish Your Body: Eat balanced, whole foods that promote your health and energy. Fueling your body properly supports a positive mindset and keeps you feeling at your best.

8. Surround Yourself with Positivity: Spend time with people who uplift you. Positive, supportive relationships are essential for cultivating an optimistic outlook.

9. Engage in Activities that Bring Joy: Pursue hobbies, passions, and creative interests that make you feel happy and fulfilled. When doing things you enjoy it nurtures your sense of well-being.

10. Connect with Your Purpose: Reflect on your values, passions, and long-term goals to give your life direction and meaning. When you know your purpose, you're more motivated to stay positive and pursue your dreams.

Go get it!

Reflection Questions:

1. What are some negative thoughts you tend to have? How can you reframe them into more optimistic perspectives?

2. Reflect on a recent challenge. How did your attitude influence the outcome? What would have happened if you approached it with a more optimistic mindset?

3. What activities or habits help you stay positive? How can you incorporate more of them into your daily routine?

4. Who in your life embodies optimism? How do they inspire you, and how can you learn from their mindset?

Action Steps:

Challenge Negative Thoughts: Every time you think "I can't," flip it to "How can I?" and brainstorm solutions.

Visualize Success: Spend time each day imagining your goals coming to fruition.

Evaluate your mastery of The Optimistic Principle. Rate Yourself 1-10 _____

Reflections

Reflections

Gratitude: Cultivate Appreciation for the Present

3. Gratitude: Cultivate Appreciation for the _____

"Gratitude is the attitude that determines our altitude."

Gratitude shifts your focus from what you don't have to what you do have. It reminds you to appreciate the small victories along the way and acknowledge the people who support you. When you practice gratitude, you shift your mindset from scarcity to abundance, making room for even more blessings.

Why It's Important: Gratitude…

_____ _____,

_____ _____ and

_____ _____.

It also enhances resilience, allowing you to handle setbacks more gracefully.

"Opportunities bring opportunities."

10 Actions to Cultivate Gratitude

Gratitude is something that can be developed through consistent practice. Here are 10 actions you can take to begin cultivating a gratitude mindset:

1. Thank Others: Verbally express your appreciation to those who help or support you. A simple "thank you" can go a long way in strengthening relationships and spreading positivity.

2. Write Thank-You Notes: Take the time to send handwritten or digital notes to express heartfelt thanks. Whether for a gift, a kind gesture, or someone's support, let others know their efforts are valued.

3. Share Gratitude with Others: Share three things you're thankful for with a friend, family member, or colleague. This can deepen your connection with others and encourage a gratitude exchange.

4. Gratitude Journal: Each day, write down a few things you are grateful for. They can be as simple as a warm cup of coffee, a productive meeting, or a kind gesture from a stranger. This practice helps train your mind to focus on the positives.

5. Gratitude Log: Keep a running list of things you're thankful for each day. This can be a quick list of bullet points that you add to over time, allowing you to look back on your gratitude journey.

6. Surprise Gifts: Surprise someone with a thoughtful gift or treat, just to show appreciation. Small gestures of kindness can have a big impact.

7. Acts of Service: Offer your help or assistance to others without expecting anything in return. Acts of service strengthen bonds and create a ripple effect of gratitude.

8. Volunteer: Give back to your community by volunteering. Helping others fosters gratitude, expands your sense of purpose, and strengthens social connections.

9. Gratitude Circle: Share things you're thankful for with your family or friends during dinner or before bed. This practice creates a space for positive reflection and mutual appreciation.

10. Daily Gratitude Meditation: Spend a few minutes each day reflecting on the things you're thankful for. A short meditation can help center your thoughts and ground you in gratitude.

Go get it!

Reflection Questions:

1. What are three things you are grateful for today?

2. How can you express gratitude to others in a way that feels meaningful to them?

3. Think about a difficult situation in your life. What lessons can you find in that experience?

4. How can you incorporate more gratitude practices into your daily routine?

Go get it!

Action Steps:

Start a Gratitude Journal: Write down three things you are thankful for each day.

Express Thanks: Reach out to someone who has impacted your life and thank them.

Evaluate your mastery of The Gratitude Principle. Rate Yourself 1-10 _____

Go get it!

Reflections

Reflections

Environments: Surround Yourself with What Fuels Your Growth

4. Environments: Surround Yourself with What Fuels Your _____

"Quality environments are the places and situations that help us grow."

Your environment shapes your experiences. The people you interact with, the places you frequent, and even the content you consume influence your mindset and behavior. A positive environment nurtures your growth, while a negative one can drain your energy.

Why It's Important: Your environment either _____ or

_____ your growth.

"Encourage means to put courage in."
-Jon Gordon

To achieve your goals, you must surround yourself with

_____

_____ and

_____ that support your vision.

10 Actions to Place Yourself in the Right Environment

Here are 10 actionable steps to ensure you're in environments that will help you grow and feel valued:

Personal Environment:

1. Self-care: Make time for activities that replenish your energy.
2. Boundary Setting: Protect your time and energy by saying no when necessary.
3. Positive Affirmations: Use affirmations to cultivate a positive mindset.

Social Environment:

4. Surround Yourself with Positivity: Spend time with uplifting people.
5. Nurture Relationships: Invest time in people who bring joy and positivity into your life.
6. Seek Mentors: Look for people who can guide and challenge you.

Professional Environment:

7. Pursue Meaningful Work: Engage in work that excites and challenges you.
8. Seek Recognition: Ask for feedback to grow and learn.
9. Develop New Skills: Invest in continuous learning to sharpen your skills.

External Environment:

10. Seek Out Supportive Communities: Engage with groups that value your contributions.

Reflection Questions:

1. What are three aspects of your personal environment that you want to improve for better growth?

2. Who in your life brings out the best in you? How can you spend more time with them?

3. Are there aspects of your professional environment that you can shift to make it more fulfilling?

4. How can you contribute to communities that align with your values?

Go get it!

Action Steps:

Assess Your Environment: Take note of your physical, mental, and social environments. Are they helping or hindering your growth?

Make Adjustments: Remove negative influences and introduce things that support your aspirations.

Evaluate your mastery of The Environment Principle. Rate Yourself 1-10 _____

Go get it!

Reflections

Reflections

Tenacity: Persevere in the Face of Challenges

5. Tenacity: Persevere in the Face of _____

"Tough times don't last, tough people do."

Tenacity is the strength to keep going even when the going gets tough. It's the relentless drive to push through obstacles, face adversity head-on, and rise above challenges. Tenacity isn't just about working hard; it's about being resilient when things don't go as planned.

"Grow Through Your Go Through."

Why It's Important: Life will test you. But if you're tenacious, you'll keep going when others give up.

Tenacity builds _____, and each challenge you overcome makes you _____

Kintsukuroi- the Japanese art of repairing broken pottery with gold, silver or platinum. When we exhibit tenacity we "repair" ourselves with the lessons learned. This makes us more valuable to have experienced the tough challenges.

10 Actions to Exhibit Tenacity

To help you develop and demonstrate tenacity in your life, here are 10 key actions to implement:

Resilience and Adaptability

1. Embrace Challenges: View every obstacle as an opportunity for growth and learning. Challenges are not roadblocks; they are steppingstones to success.

2. Stay Flexible: Adapt to new situations and changes in plans. Life rarely goes as expected, so being flexible allows you to keep going despite setbacks.

3. Learn from Failures: Instead of seeing failure as defeat, analyze it. What can you learn from this setback? Use these lessons to adjust and improve.

Goal-Oriented Mindset

4. Set Clear Goals: Break your larger vision down into specific, achievable objectives. This keeps you focused and motivated.

5. Chunking: Break them down into manageable tasks that you can tackle a few at a time.

6. Track Progress: Keep a record of your progress. Celebrate small victories to maintain motivation. Adjust strategies when needed.

Self-Discipline and Motivation

7. Create a Schedule and Stick to It: Consistency is key. Create a schedule that aligns with your goals and stick to it—even on tough days.

8. Find Your "Why": Identify what motivates you and keep it at the forefront of your mind. Remind yourself why you started, especially when times get tough.

9. Celebrate Small Wins: Acknowledge and celebrate every step forward, no matter how small. This helps keep the momentum going.

10. Surround Yourself with Supportive People: Share your goals and progress with trusted individuals who can encourage, support, and hold you accountable.

Go get it!

Reflection Questions:

1. Think of a recent challenge. How did you handle it? What could you do differently next time to show more tenacity?

2. What is one goal that requires your tenacity? What's one small action you can take today to move closer to it?

3. Who can you lean on for support and accountability? How will you involve them in your journey toward success?

Go get it!

Action Steps:

Set Short-Term Milestones: Break your big goals into smaller, manageable steps to maintain momentum.

Embrace Failure as Learning: When you face setbacks, ask yourself, "What did I learn from this?"

Evaluate your mastery of The Tenacity Principle. Rate Yourself 1-10 _____

Go get it!

Reflections

Reflections

Intentions: Live with Clarity and Purpose

6. Intentions: Live with _____ and

_____

"Pure hearted intentions lead to pure actions."

Intentions guide your actions and ensure that your efforts are aligned with your

_____ _____ and long-term _____.

Living intentionally means doing things with purpose and focusing your energy on what truly matters.

Why It's Important: When your actions are intentional, you stay on track toward your goals and avoid _____ that can derail you.

"Where your focus goes, your energy flows."
"Where your energy flows, your focus goes."

10 Actions to Help You Exhibit Pure Intentions

Living with pure-hearted intentions is not a passive endeavor—it requires intentional actions. Here are 10 steps to help you align your intentions with authenticity, clarity, and purpose:

Self-Reflection and Awareness

1. Examine Your Motivations: Regularly take a step back and reflect on why you're doing what you're doing. Are your actions aligned with your values and purpose?

2. Recognize Biases and Assumptions: Be aware of your own biases. Try to consider alternative perspectives and avoid making snap judgments.

Honesty and Transparency

3. Communicate Openly and Truthfully: Share your thoughts, feelings, and intentions clearly. Honesty creates trust and fosters understanding.

4. Be Transparent in Your Actions: Ensure your actions align with your words. When you act with transparency, others will see your true intentions.

Empathy and Compassion

5. Consider the Impact on Others: Think about how your actions will affect those around you. Will they bring harm, or will they uplift others?

6. Practice Active Listening: When engaging with others, listen not only to respond but to understand their thoughts and emotions.

Accountability and Integrity

7. Take Responsibility for Your Actions: Own your mistakes and take the necessary steps to make amends when necessary.

8. Stay True to Your Values: Ensure that every action you take is in alignment with your personal values, even when faced with challenges.

Humility and Selflessness

9. Let Go of Ego and Selfish Desires: Prioritize the greater good over personal gain. True intentions come from a place of selflessness.

10. Seek Feedback and Constructive Criticism: Be open to learning and growth. Feedback helps refine our intentions and actions.

Reflection Questions:

1. Reflect on a recent action you took. Was it driven by pure-hearted intentions? If not, what could you change to align it with your values?

2. Think about someone you admire for their pure-hearted intentions. What qualities do they embody that you can incorporate into your own life?

3. How can you improve your self-awareness and regularly assess your motivations to ensure your actions align with your intentions?

Go get it!

Action Steps:

Set Clear Goals: Write down your top goals for the year. What do you want to achieve, and why?

Align Your Actions: Make sure that every action you take is aligned with your bigger vision.

Evaluate your mastery of The Intentions Principle. Rate Yourself 1-10 _____

Reflections

Reflections

Trust: Believe in Yourself and the Process

Go get it!

7. Trust: Believe in Yourself and the _____

Trust is the final piece of the puzzle.

Trust in _____,

trust in _____, and

trust in the _____.

When you trust, you open yourself up to new experiences, relationships, and opportunities. Trust allows you to let go of control and have faith that things will work out for the best.

"Control the controllables, don't worry about the things you can't control."

Why It's Important: Trust allows you to be _____, _____ _____, and be open to the _____.

It helps you navigate life's uncertainties with confidence.

"Reps make you better."

10 Actions to Demonstrate Trustworthiness

Building trust takes consistent effort and a commitment to honesty, empathy, and reliability. Here are 10 key actions to help you demonstrate trustworthiness:

Reliability and Accountability

1. Follow Through on Commitments: Always meet deadlines and fulfill promises. Being consistent in your actions builds trust.

2. Take Responsibility: Own up to mistakes and make amends when necessary. Accountability fosters trust and respect.

3. Be Transparent: Share information openly and explain your actions clearly to ensure transparency in all dealings.

Honesty and Integrity

4. Be Truthful: Always speak truthfully, even when it's difficult. Honesty is a critical component of trust.

5. Avoid Gossip: Refrain from sharing confidential or unverified information. Respecting others' privacy builds trust.

6. Keep Confidences: When someone confides in you, protect their trust by maintaining confidentiality.

Empathy and Understanding

7. Listen Actively: Engage fully with others and understand their perspectives before reacting. Active listening promotes trust.

8. Show Empathy: Demonstrate understanding and compassion towards others. Empathy deepens relationships and trust.

Consistency and Dependability

9. Be Consistent: Maintain a steady approach in both your behavior and decisions. Predictability in your actions builds trust.

10. Follow Through on Promises: Ensure that your actions align with your words. Reliability in fulfilling promises is the foundation of trust.

Go get it!

Reflection Questions:

1. Reflect on a situation where someone's trust in you helped you grow. How did their belief in you impact your actions and confidence?

2. Think about a recent commitment you made. Did you follow through on it? If not, what can you do next time to ensure you build trust by honoring your promises?

3. When was the last time you were vulnerable with someone? How did that vulnerability strengthen the relationship and increase mutual trust?

Go get it!

Action Steps:

Build Self-Confidence: Reflect on your past successes and trust that you can handle whatever comes your way.

Trust the Timing: Believe that everything is happening for a reason, and trust that the God has a plan for you.

Evaluate your mastery of The Trust Principle. Rate Yourself 1-10 _____

Reflections

Reflections

Putting It All Together

The **G.O.G.E.T.I.T. Blueprint** is a roadmap for living a _____. It's a daily commitment to stay grounded, embrace optimism, practice gratitude, create empowering environments, be tenacious, act with purpose, and trust in the journey. Each of these principles work together to create the life you've always dreamed of.

As you go out into the world, remember this:

You are _____,

you are _____, and

you are ready to go get it!

Your legacy is waiting for you to take _____!

Go get it!

Reflections

Reflections

Reflection and Action Plan

1. Which of the G.O.G.E.T.I.T. principles do you feel most aligned with right now and why?

2. Where do you need to focus more energy to create a stronger foundation for your legacy?

3. Write down one action step you will take today to move forward with clarity and purpose in building your legacy.

Go get it!

The Go Get It Principles

G - Grounded: Stay Rooted in Your Values and Principles

O - Optimistic: Embrace a Mindset of Possibility

G - Gratitude: Cultivate Appreciation for the Present

E - Environments: Surround Yourself with What Fuels Your Growth

T - Tenacity: Persevere in the Face of Challenges

I - Intentions: Live with Clarity and Purpose

T - Trust: Believe in Yourself and the Process

About The Author

Chip Baker is a fourth-generation educator. He has been a teacher/coach for over twenty-six years. He is a multiple time best-selling Author, Youtuber/Podcaster, Transformational Speaker and Life Coach.

Chip Baker is the creator of the YouTube channel/podcast "Chip Baker - The Success Chronicles" where he interviews people from all walks of life and shares their stories for positive inspiration and motivation.

Live. Learn. Serve. Inspire. Go get it!

Social Media:
Email: chipbakertsc@gmail.com
Wrote By Me: https://www.wroteby.me/chipbaker
Online Store: http://chip-baker-the-success-chronicles.square.site/
Facebook: https://www.facebook.com/profile.php?id=100014641035295
Instagram: @chipbakertsc
LinkedIn: http://linkedin.com/in/chip-baker-thesuccesschronicles-825887161
X: @chipbaker19
Chip Baker-The Success Chronicles
YouTube:
youtube.com/c/ChipBakerTheSuccessChronicles
Podcast: https://anchor.fm/chip-baker

Chip Baker Books:

Growing Through Your Go Through
Effective Conversation to Ignite Relationships
Suited For Success Vol. 2
The Formula Chart for Life
The Impact of Influence
R.O.C.K. Solid
The Impact of Influence Vol. 2
Kids Book- Stay On The Right P.A.T.H.
The Impact of Influence Vol. 3

Black Men Love
The Impact of Influence Vol. 4
The Winning Mindset
The Impact of Influence Vol. 5
Concrete Connections
The Impact of Influence Vol. 6
Voices For Leadership: Embracing Diverse Strategies for Effective Leadership
Sole Searching: Daily Devotional for Sneakerheads
It's Not About Me
The Impact of Influence Vol. 7
The Impact of Influence Vol. 8
Destiny to Dallas
The Impact of Influence Vol. 9
The Impact of Influence Vol. 10
The Impact of Influence, Compilation of Chip Baker Chapters
Go Get It, 7 Principles to Live a Legacy
G.A.M.E.- Generational Applicable Messages for Everyone
Teacher

Online Store

Answers

Chapter Blanks

The Power of Go Get It

legacy
purpose
fulfillment
lasting
impact
foundation
success
greatness

Grounded: Stay Rooted in Your Values and Principles

Values
Principles
clarity
stability
strength
long
term
goals

Optimistic: Embrace a Mindset of Possibility

Mindset
belief
solution
unclear
opportunities
motivated

Gratitude: Cultivate Appreciation for the Present

Present
Increases

happiness
reduces
stress
improves
relationships

Environments: Surround Yourself with What Fuels Your Growth

Growth
encourages
hinders
people
places
activities

Tenacity: Persevere in the Face of Challenges

Challenges
character
stronger

Intentions: Live with Clarity and Purpose

Clarity
Purpose
core
values
goals
distractions

Trust: Believe in Yourself and the Process

Process
yourself
others
process
vulnerable
take
risks

future

Putting it All Together

legacy
capable
worthy
action

Made in the USA
Coppell, TX
20 January 2026

68842328R00046